W9-AZG-401

Pebble® Plus

Health and Your Body

Healthy Habits

by Rebecca Weber

CAPSTONE PRESS
a capstone imprint

Pebble Plus is published by Capstone Press,
151 Good Counsel Drive, P.O. Box 669, Mankato, Minnesota 56002.
www.capstonepub.com

Books published by Capstone Press are manufactured with paper
containing at least 10 percent post-consumer waste.

Library of Congress Cataloging-in-Publication Data
Weber, Rebecca.
  Healthy habits / by Rebecca Weber.
     p. cm. — (Pebble plus. Health and your body)
  Includes bibliographical references and index.
  ISBN 978-1-4296-6611-4 (library binding)
  1. Health—Juvenile literature. 2. Health behavior—Juvenile
literature. I. Title.
  RA777.W43 2011
  613—dc22   2010034313

Summary: Simple text and color photos illustrate ways to stay healthy through exercise, rest, skin care, and proper diet.

Editorial Credits
Gillia Olson, editor; Veronica Correia, designer; Svetlana Zhurkin, media researcher;
     Laura Manthe, production specialist

Photo Credits
BananaStock, 1, 11, 19
Capstone Press/Hutchings Photography, 20
Capstone Studio/Karon Dubke, 17
Dreamstime/Yobro10, 21
Shutterstock: AVAVA, 9; Jaimie Duplass, 15; Larisa Lofitskaya, 7; Martin Valigursky, 5; Monkey Business Images, cover;
     Paulaphoto, 13

Note to Parents and Teachers

The Health and Your Body series supports national standards related to health and physical
education. This book describes and illustrates how to stay healthy. The images support early
readers in understanding the text. The repetition of words and phrases helps early readers learn
new words. This book also introduces early readers to subject-specific vocabulary words, which are
defined in the Glossary section. Early readers may need assistance to read some words and to use
the Table of Contents, Glossary, Read More, Internet Sites, and Index sections of the book.

Printed in the United States of America in North Mankato, Minnesota.
092010
005933CGS11

Table of Contents

A Healthy Day

Our bodies need things every day to stay healthy. The right foods, enough sleep, and exercise are all important.

How can you be healthy today?

Good Food

Your body needs energy from breakfast to start the day. Fruit will give you energy fast. Eggs and milk will give you energy for hours.

Clean and Shiny

Wash your skin to get rid
of germs and dirt.
Use warm water and soap.
Wear sunscreen outside to
protect your skin from the sun.

Teeth Talk

Brush your teeth at least

two times every day.

Brush after eating sweets too.

Use dental floss to get rid of

food between your teeth.

Playing Hard

Exercise makes strong muscles.

Play games with your friends.

Run, jump, or swim.

Get moving for at least

30 minutes a day. Have fun!

13

Don't Dry Out

Your body needs water more
than food or anything else.
Thirst means your body is
already low on water.
Drink water throughout the day.

Snack Attack

Healthy snacks give you energy all day long. Energy from chips and candy doesn't last. Eat nuts or cheese for energy that lasts a long time.

Deep Sleep

Even after a healthy day, your body needs rest to repair itself. Most kids need about 10 hours of sleep a day. Good rest ends a full day of healthy habits.

Fun Facts

- People have not always had toothpaste. They used to brush their teeth with ground up chalk, ashes, or even baking soda.

- Fresh fruits and vegetables have more vitamins than frozen. Frozen fruits and vegetables have more vitamins than canned.

- Strong muscles don't just help you play longer. They can help keep your body from getting hurt while you play.

- The average adult has about 8 pounds (3.6 kilograms) of skin. People shed skin cells all the time. The body grows entirely new skin about once every 35 days.

- People spend about one-third of their life sleeping. Dreams happen during rapid eye movement (REM) sleep. During this time, our eyes dart back and forth under our eyelids.

Glossary

dental floss—a thin strand of thread used to clean in between teeth

energy—the strength to do active things without becoming tired

exercise—physical activity that a person does to stay fit and healthy

germ—a very tiny living thing that can cause sickness

habit—something you do regularly, often without thinking about it

repair—to fix

sunscreen—a lotion that protects your skin from the sun

Read More

Hallinan, P. K. *Let's Be Fit.* Nashville, Tenn.: Ideals Children's Books, 2007.

Rissman, Rebecca. *My Food Pyramid.* Healthy Eating. Chicago: Heinemann Library, 2011.

Rockwell, Lizzy. *The Busy Body Book: A Kid's Guide to Fitness.* New York: Dragonfly Books, 2008.

Internet Sites

FactHound offers a safe, fun way to find Internet sites related to this book. All of the sites on FactHound have been researched by our staff.

Here's all you do:

Visit *www.facthound.com*

Type in this code: 9781429666114

Super-cool stuff!

Check out projects, games and lots more at
www.capstonekids.com

Index

Word Count: 205 (main text)
Grade: 1
Early-Intervention Level: 20